VOLUME TWO

TEXAS LORE

by Patrick M. Reynolds

Published by

THE RED ROSE STUDIO

Willow Street, Pennsylvania 17584

To My Daughter, Maria Alyssa

ISBN 0-932514-09-X

Printed In The U.S.A.

Contents

Special Thanks

Several people deserve to be recognized for helping me with some of the research for **Texas Lore.**

Mrs. Virginia Ming, The Texas Collection, Baylor University, Waco, TX for her prompt and excellent cooperation in gathering and sending me hard-to-find bits of information, portraits and photos for many stories in this book.

Hon. Scott Bailey, Judge of Eastland County, TX. (Old Rip, The Cisco Santa)

Prof. F. E. Abernethy, Secretary-Editor, Texas Folklore Society, Stephen F. Austin University, Nacogdoches, TX. (The Cottonwood Claim, The Headless Ghost, Stampede Mesa, The Great Western)

Wayne Daniel, Librarian-Archivist, Fort Concho National Historic Landmark, San Angelo, TX. (Andrew Jackson Porter, The Fighting Parson)

Texas Parks & Wildlife Department, Austin, TX. (Kreische's Brewery, Fort Lancaster)

Chuck Livolsi, Pittsburgh, PA; John B. Roda, Lancaster, PA; and Mike Petronella, River Edge, NJ for assisting me with some of the artwork.

The **Texas Lore** stories in this book appeared (weekly) in the following fine newspapers between July, 1983 and July, 1984:

Bastrop County Times
Brazosport Facts
Bryan-College Station Eagle
Corpus Christi Ad Sack
Dallas Morning News
Hondo Anvil Herald
Houston Post
Kingsville Record
Northwest (San Antonio) Leader
Odessa American
Pharr Press
Zavala County Sentinel

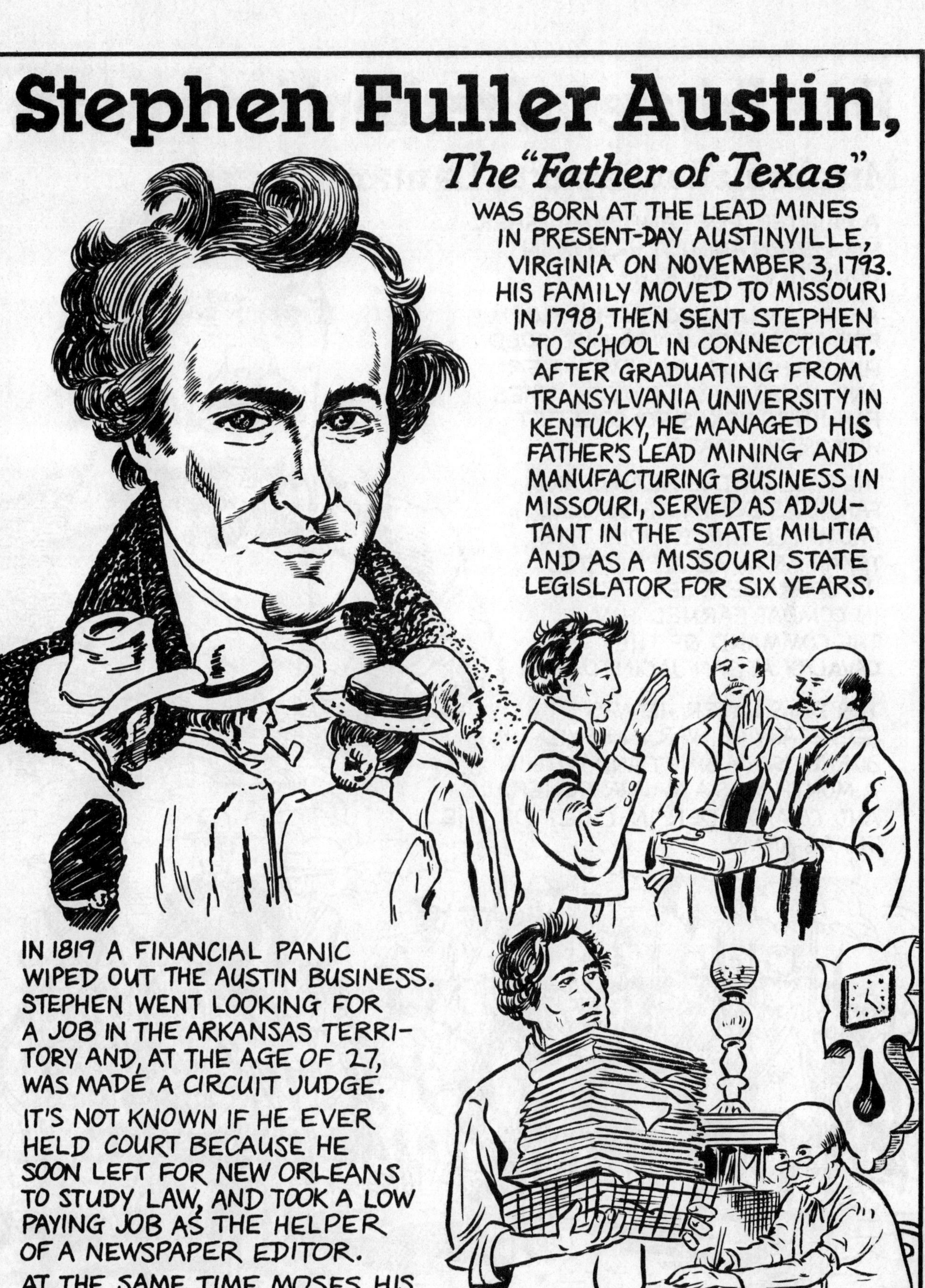
Stephen Fuller Austin,
The "Father of Texas"
WAS BORN AT THE LEAD MINES IN PRESENT-DAY AUSTINVILLE, VIRGINIA ON NOVEMBER 3, 1793. HIS FAMILY MOVED TO MISSOURI IN 1798, THEN SENT STEPHEN TO SCHOOL IN CONNECTICUT. AFTER GRADUATING FROM TRANSYLVANIA UNIVERSITY IN KENTUCKY, HE MANAGED HIS FATHER'S LEAD MINING AND MANUFACTURING BUSINESS IN MISSOURI, SERVED AS ADJUTANT IN THE STATE MILITIA AND AS A MISSOURI STATE LEGISLATOR FOR SIX YEARS.
IN 1819 A FINANCIAL PANIC WIPED OUT THE AUSTIN BUSINESS. STEPHEN WENT LOOKING FOR A JOB IN THE ARKANSAS TERRITORY AND, AT THE AGE OF 27, WAS MADE A CIRCUIT JUDGE.
IT'S NOT KNOWN IF HE EVER HELD COURT BECAUSE HE SOON LEFT FOR NEW ORLEANS TO STUDY LAW, AND TOOK A LOW PAYING JOB AS THE HELPER OF A NEWSPAPER EDITOR.
AT THE SAME TIME MOSES, HIS FATHER, CONCEIVED A PLAN TO COLONIZE TEXAS—AN IDEA STEPHEN THOUGHT RIDICULOUS.

From Private to President in two years
Mirabeau Buonaparte Lamar
A PAINTER, POET AND PUBLISHER WAS BORN AUGUST 16, 1798 IN LOUISVILLE, GEORGIA.
AFTER AN UNSUCCESSFUL RUN FOR CONGRESS IN 1834 HE SOLD HIS COLUMBUS (GA.) *ENQUIRER* AND, IN 1835, FOLLOWED JAMES FANNIN TO TEXAS TO COLLECT HISTORICAL DATA.
THE FALL OF THE ALAMO AND FANNIN'S DEATH AT GOLIAD PROMPTED HIM TO JOIN THE TEXAS ARMY AS A PRIVATE. HIS COURAGE & LEADERSHIP IN COMBAT EARNED HIM THE COMMAND OF THE CAVALRY AT SAN JACINTO.
TEN DAYS LATER HE WAS SECRETARY OF WAR IN DAVID BURNET'S CABINET AND WITHIN A MONTH WAS A MAJOR GENERAL AND COMMANDER-IN-CHIEF OF THE TEXAS ARMY.
A FIERY POLITICIAN
LAMAR SUCCEEDED SAM HOUSTON AS PRESIDENT OF TEXAS IN 1838.

WHEN CONSTRUCTION OF THE STATE CAPITOL WAS NEARING COMPLETION IN 1888 IT WAS DECIDED TO TOP OFF THE DOME WITH A ZINC STATUE OF
the Goddess of Liberty.
THE FIGURE WAS CAST IN SECTIONS AND PIECED TOGETHER ON THE CAPITOL GROUNDS, THEN HOISTED INTO PLACE. THE UNKNOWN SCULPTOR GAVE HER EXAGGERATED FEATURES SO THAT WHEN VIEWED FROM THE STREETS OF AUSTIN SHE LOOKS BEAUTIFUL.
THE DIRECTION SHE FACES WAS STRONGLY SUGGESTED BY SOME CONFEDERATE WAR VETERANS:
...DON'T MATTER WHERE SHE FACES AS LONG AS HER BACKSIDE FACES NORTH!

Friar Morfi's Diary

IN 1777 FRIAR JUAN AGUSTIN MORFI WENT WITH COMMANDANT GENERAL DE CROIX ON A TOUR OF THE PROVINCES MAKING NOTES IN HIS DIARY. HE VISITED TEXAS AND LATER WROTE ONE OF THE FIRST HISTORIES OF THE AREA. NOT MUCH ESCAPED HIS KEEN EYE INCLUDING SOME INCIDENTS THAT WERE EMBARRASSING TO HIM.

FRIAR MORFI LOVED TO FISH. ONE DAY HE AND TWO OF DE CROIX'S OFFICERS DECIDED TO FISH IN THE SAN ANTONIO RIVER. WALKING ACROSS SAN ANTONIO'S MUDDY PLAZA THEY CAME UPON A STRAY BULL. THE BULL WANTED THE PLACE TO HIMSELF SO HE CHARGED & THE THREE ANGLERS RAN FOR THEIR LIVES.

ON HIS WAY BACK TO MEXICO HE STOPPED TO FISH IN THE RIO GRANDE AND FELL IN. MORFI MUST HAVE GOTTEN LOST BECAUSE HIS DIARY ENDS ABRUPTLY AT LAS CRUCES, N. MEX. ON FEB. 24, 1778. HE FINALLY SHOWED UP IN MEXICO A MONTH LATER.

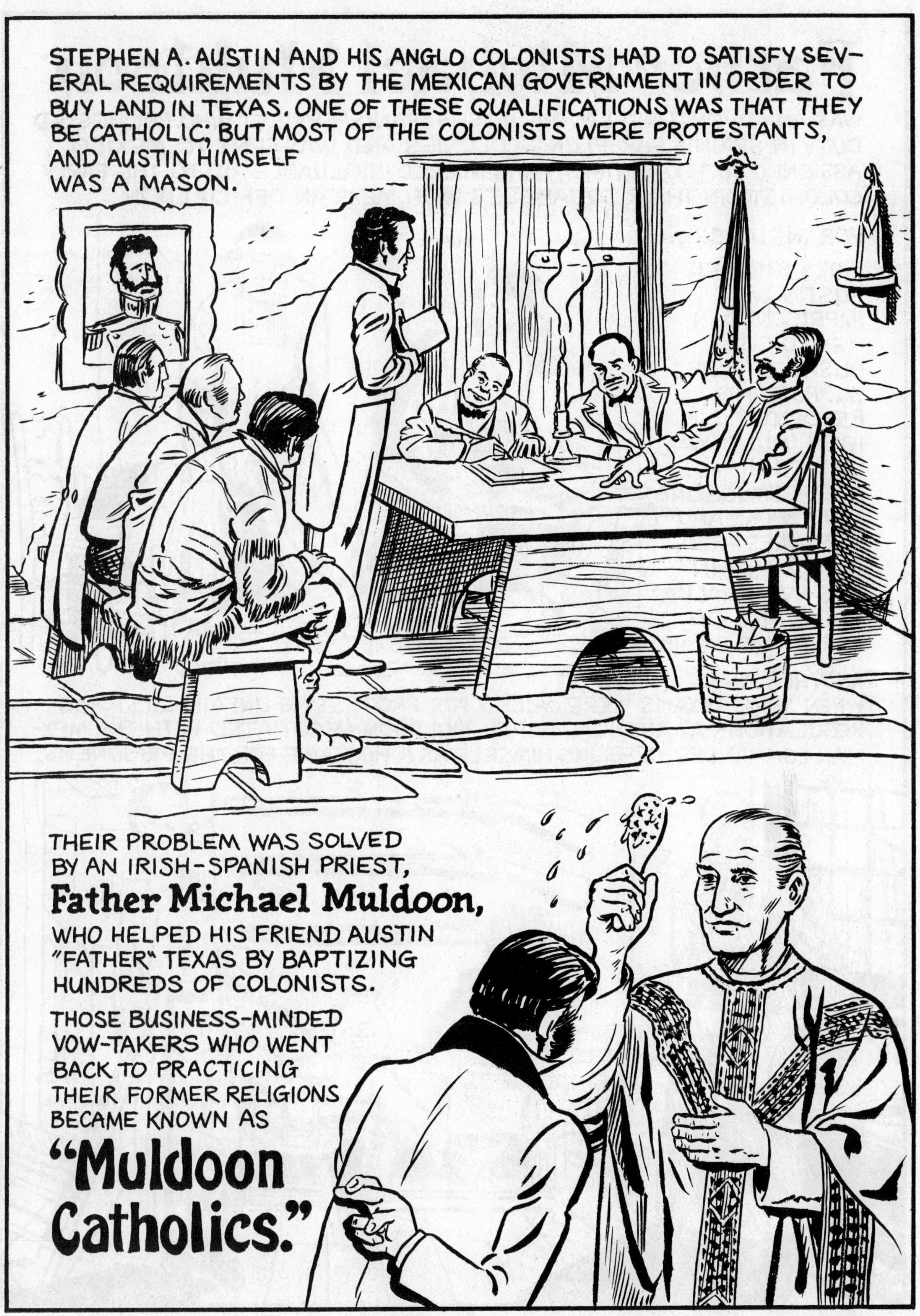
STEPHEN A. AUSTIN AND HIS ANGLO COLONISTS HAD TO SATISFY SEV-
ERAL REQUIREMENTS BY THE MEXICAN GOVERNMENT IN ORDER TO
BUY LAND IN TEXAS. ONE OF THESE QUALIFICATIONS WAS THAT THEY
BE CATHOLIC; BUT MOST OF THE COLONISTS WERE PROTESTANTS,
AND AUSTIN HIMSELF
WAS A MASON.
THEIR PROBLEM WAS SOLVED
BY AN IRISH-SPANISH PRIEST,
Father Michael Muldoon,
WHO HELPED HIS FRIEND AUSTIN
"FATHER" TEXAS BY BAPTIZING
HUNDREDS OF COLONISTS.
THOSE BUSINESS-MINDED
VOW-TAKERS WHO WENT
BACK TO PRACTICING
THEIR FORMER RELIGIONS
BECAME KNOWN AS
"Muldoon
Catholics."

Father Michael Muldoon

WAS AN ADVENTURE-LOVING IRISH-SPANISH PRIEST WHO REQUESTED DUTY IN SPAIN'S FAR-FLUNG COLONIES AND WAS SENT TO MEXICO. ASSIGNED TO TEXAS IN 1829, HE RENDERED INVALUABLE AID TO THE EARLY COLONISTS IN THEIR SQUABBLES WITH MEXICAN OFFICIALDOM.

FOR INSTANCE...

WHEN STEPHEN AUSTIN WAS IMPRISONED IN MEXICO CITY SUSPECTED OF SUPPORTING REVOLUTION IN 1834, MULDOON VISITED HIM THERE, SMUGGLING FOOD, BOOKS AND MESSAGES FROM TEXAS. AUSTIN WAS EVENTUALLY RELEASED ON CHRISTMAS DAY, 1834.

ANOTHER TIME,
WHEN SOME TEXANS WERE JAILED FOR PROTESTING UNFAIR CUSTOMS REGULATIONS AT ANAHUAC IN 1831, MULDOON NEGOTIATED WITH THE MEXICAN COMMANDER, OFFERING HIMSELF AS A HOSTAGE FOR THE PRISONERS.

The Further Adventures of Father Mike Muldoon

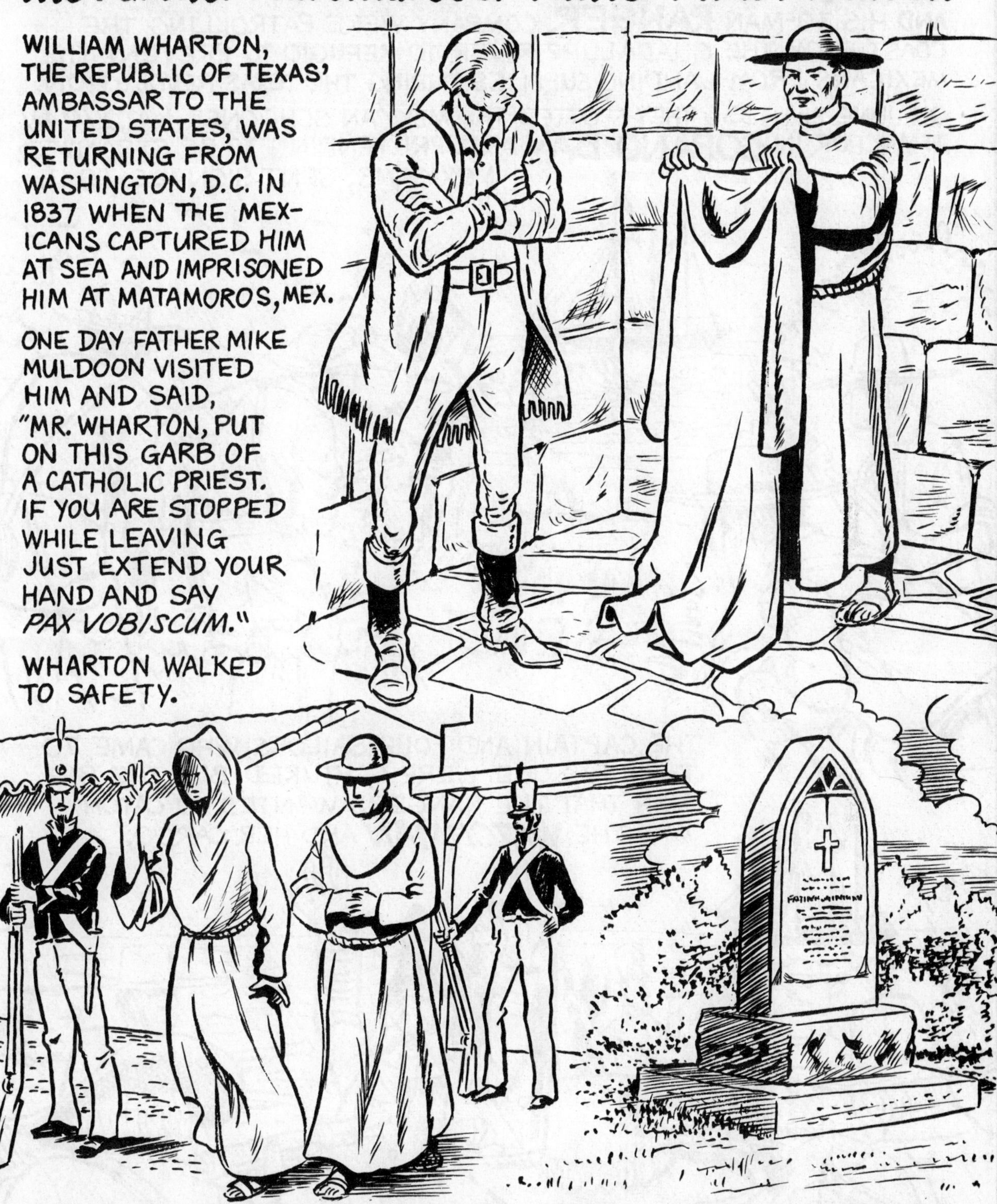

TWO YEARS LATER FR. MULDOON WENT BACK TO MEXICO. SANTA ANNA, INFORMED OF HIS EXPLOITS ON BEHALF OF THE TEXANS, WAITED. THE PRIEST WAS NEVER HEARD FROM AGAIN.

TODAY A TOWN IN FAYETTE CO. IS NAMED AFTER MULDOON. ON RT. 77 NEAR SCHULENBERG STANDS THIS MONUMENT TO AN HEROIC PADRE.

Major Isaac Watts Burton

AND HIS 30-MAN RANGER COMPANY WERE PATROLLING THE COAST FROM THE GUADALUPE RIVER TO REFUGIO TO PREVENT THE MEXICANS FROM LANDING SUPPLIES DURING THE TEXAS REVOLUTION.

ON JUNE 2nd, 1836 THEY SPOTTED THE MEXICAN SCHOONER *WATCHMAN* AT ANCHOR IN **COPANO BAY** AND, PRETENDING TO BE STRANDED MEXICANS, SENT SIGNALS TO IT.

Surprise! Surprise!

AFTER CAPTURING A MEXICAN NAVY CAPTAIN AND FOUR CREW MEMBERS MAJOR BURTON AND SIXTEEN OF HIS RANGERS ROWED THE MEXICANS' BOAT TO THE SCHOONER ***WATCHMAN*** IN **COPANO BAY.**

THE MEXICAN CREW, MISTAKING THE TEXANS FOR COMRADES, PERMITTED THEM TO BOARD. CAUGHT OFF GUARD THE MEXICANS SURRENDERED IMMEDIATELY.

THE SHIP WAS LADEN WITH MILITARY SUPPLIES.

BURTON PREPARED TO SEND THE SHIP TO VELASCO AS A **PRIZE** OF WAR BUT UNFAVORABLE WINDS DELAYED THEM FOR TWO WEEKS.

THIS DONE, THE TEXAS RANGERS AGAIN SEIZED TWO MORE SHIPS WITHOUT A FIGHT. THEN TURNED EVERYTHING OVER TO THEIR COUNTRYMEN, FIRST AT VELASCO THEN AT GALVESTON.

THIS INCIDENT GAINED MAJ. BURTON & HIS BOYS INSTANT FAME AS

The Horse Marines.

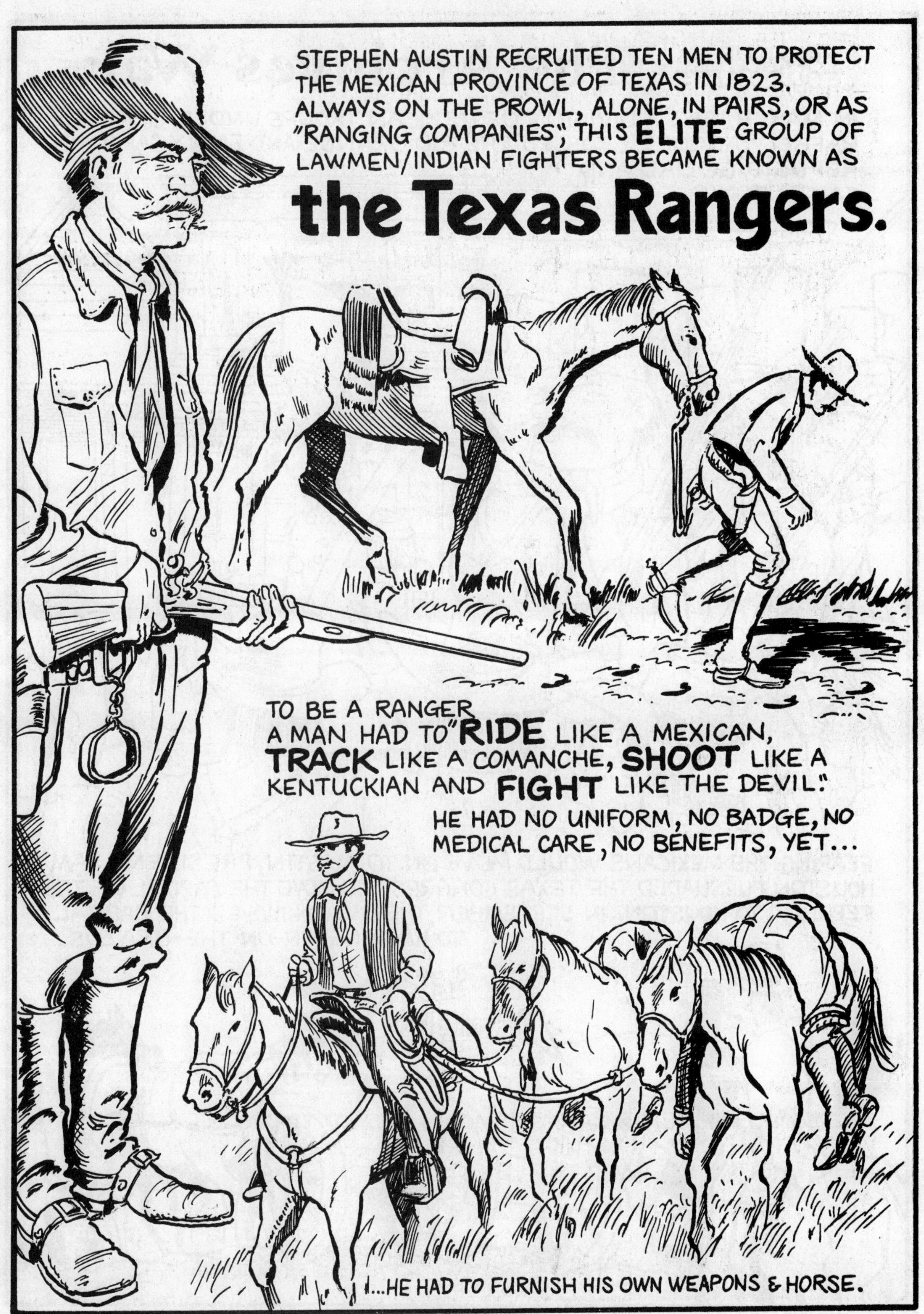
STEPHEN AUSTIN RECRUITED TEN MEN TO PROTECT THE MEXICAN PROVINCE OF TEXAS IN 1823. ALWAYS ON THE PROWL, ALONE, IN PAIRS, OR AS "RANGING COMPANIES", THIS ELITE GROUP OF LAWMEN/INDIAN FIGHTERS BECAME KNOWN AS
the Texas Rangers.
TO BE A RANGER A MAN HAD TO "RIDE LIKE A MEXICAN, TRACK LIKE A COMANCHE, SHOOT LIKE A KENTUCKIAN AND FIGHT LIKE THE DEVIL."
HE HAD NO UNIFORM, NO BADGE, NO MEDICAL CARE, NO BENEFITS, YET...
...HE HAD TO FURNISH HIS OWN WEAPONS & HORSE.

FIRST OF FOUR PARTS

The Archives War

IN MARCH, 1842 A DIVISION OF MEXICAN TROOPS UNDER GENERAL RAFAEL VASQUEZ CROSSED THE RIO GRANDE AND EASILY CAPTURED REFUGIO, GOLIAD AND SAN ANTONIO.

FEARING THE MEXICANS WOULD MOVE ON TO AUSTIN, PRESIDENT SAM HOUSTON PURSUADED THE TEXAS CONGRESS TO MOVE THE CAPITAL OF THE REPUBLIC TO HOUSTON. IN SEPTEMBER THEY AGAIN MOVED THE CAPITAL TO WASHINGTON-ON-THE-BRAZOS.

SECOND OF FOUR PARTS

The Archives War

MEANWHILE THE CITIZENS OF AUSTIN BELIEVED THAT THE PRESIDENT WAS GOING TO MAKE HOUSTON THE PERMANENT CAPITAL OF TEXAS. TO KEEP THIS FROM HAPPENING THEY FORMED A VIGILANCE COMMITTEE WHO LOADED THE ARCHIVES INTO CRATES AND PUT A GUARD OVER THEM.

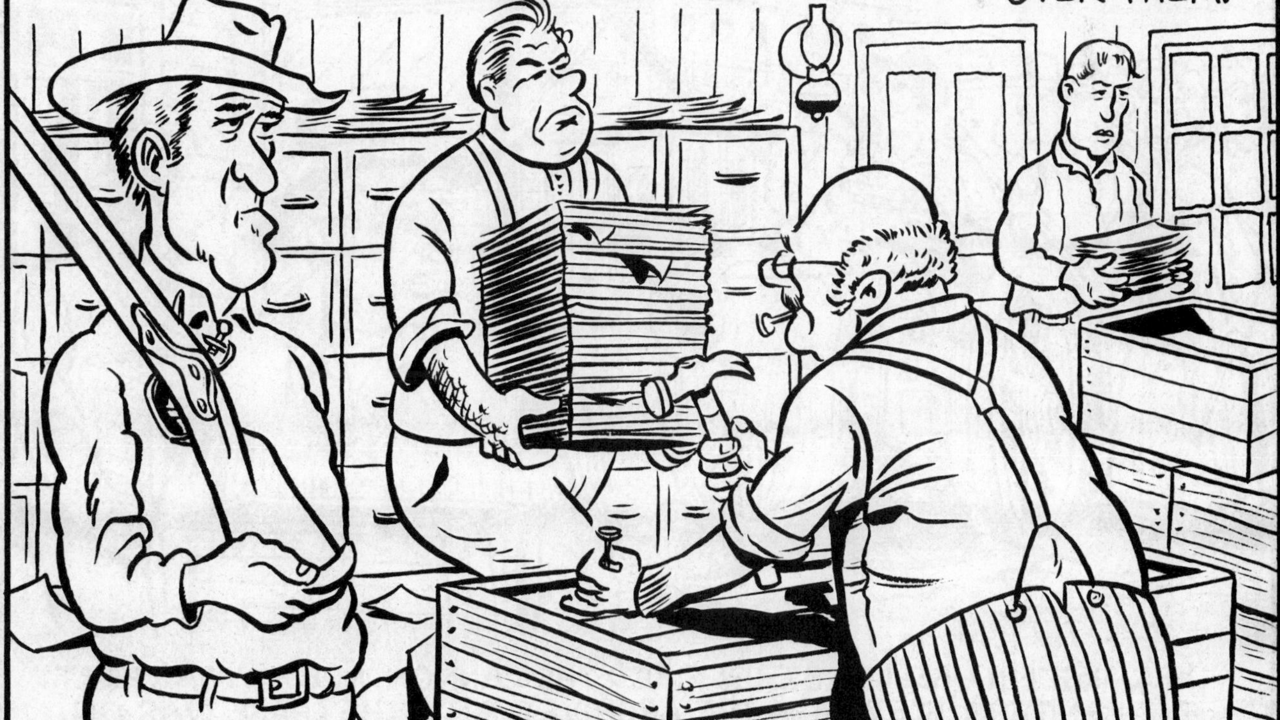

THIRD OF FOUR PARTS

The Archives War

ON DEC. 31, 1842, WHILE THE AUSTINITES WERE CELEBRATING NEW YEAR'S EVE, TWENTY RANGERS UNDER CAPTAINS SMITH AND CHANDLER SLIPPED INTO AUSTIN, SURPRISED AND DISARMED THE VIGILANTES GUARDING THE ARCHIVES AND BEGAN TO LOAD THEM INTO WAGONS.

SOME PASSERSBY NOTICED THE COMMOTION AND SOUNDED THE ALARM. HUNDREDS OF PEOPLE ARMED TO THE TEETH AND MUSTERING A FIELD GUN LOADED WITH GRAPE SHOT CAME A-RUNNING.

MRS. ANGELINA BELLE EBERLY FIRED THE CANNON. NOBODY WAS HURT. THE RANGERS FLED WITH THE ARCHIVES AND THE CHASE WAS ON.

LAST OF FOUR PARTS

The Archives War

ABOUT 20 TEXAS RANGERS WERE TRANSFERRING THE REPUBLIC'S ARCHIVES FROM AUSTIN TO HOUSTON FOR SAFE-KEEPING WHEN THEY WERE ATTACKED BY HUNDREDS OF CITIZENS WHO WANTED THE DOCUMENTS TO STAY PUT. WITH THE AUSTINITES IN HOT PURSUIT THE RANGERS REACHED KENNEY'S FORT AT BRUSHY CREEK ON NEW YEAR'S DAY, 1843.

THAT EVENING CPT. MARK B. LEWIS AND HIS POSSE OF VIGILANTES, MANY OF WHOM WERE BAREFOOTED BOYS, CAUGHT UP WITH AND SURROUNDED THE RANGERS AT THEIR CAMPSITE AT KENNEY'S FORT IN WILLIAMSON COUNTY. LEWIS DEMANDED THE RANGERS HAND OVER THE ARCHIVES.

PRESIDENT HOUSTON HAD ORDERED THE RANGERS TO AVOID BLOODSHED, SO THEY GAVE UP THE ARCHIVES. LEWIS' PEOPLE HAULED THEM BACK TO AUSTIN WHERE THEY REMAIN TO THIS DAY-UNMOLESTED.

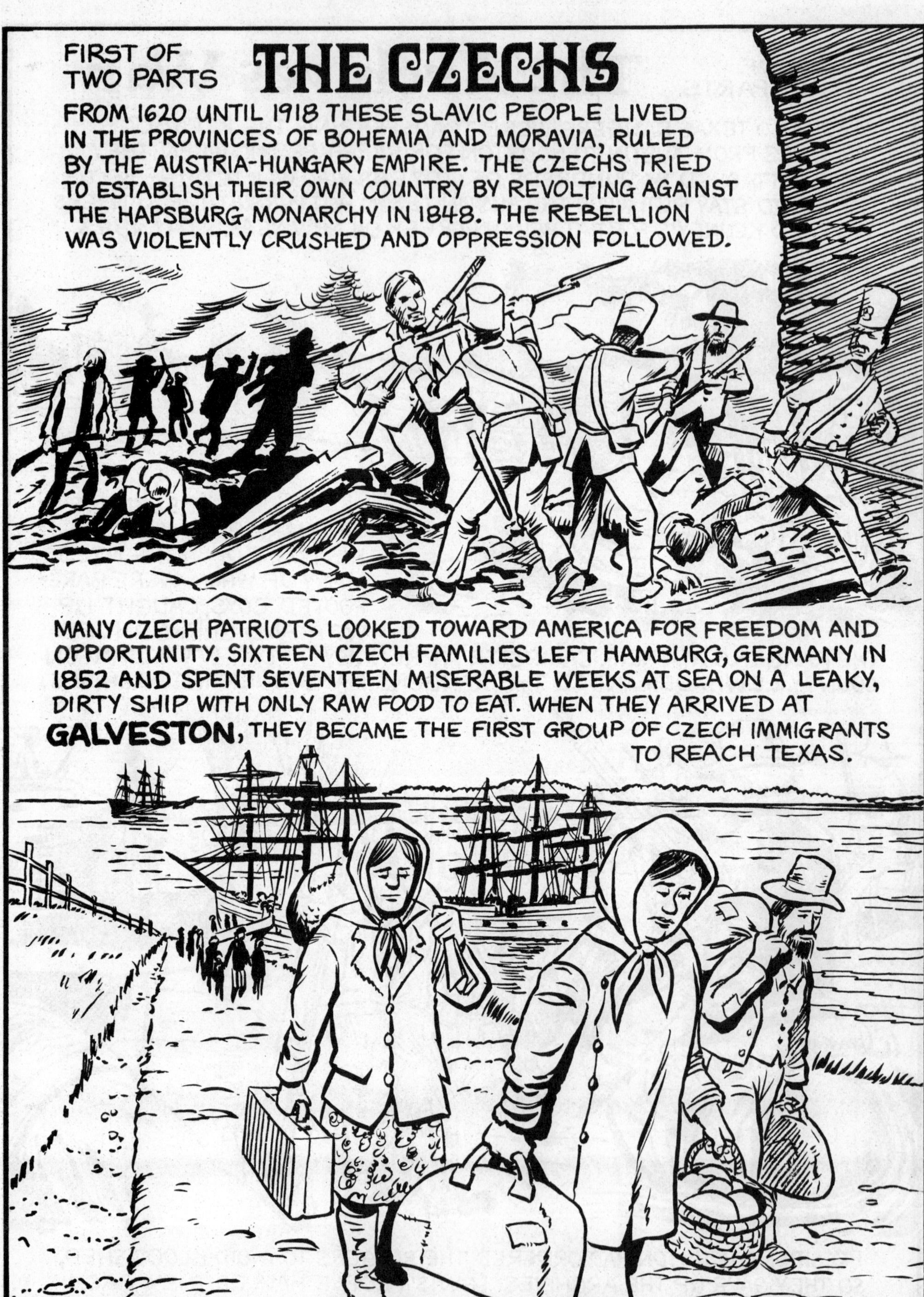
FIRST OF TWO PARTS
THE CZECHS
FROM 1620 UNTIL 1918 THESE SLAVIC PEOPLE LIVED IN THE PROVINCES OF BOHEMIA AND MORAVIA, RULED BY THE AUSTRIA-HUNGARY EMPIRE. THE CZECHS TRIED TO ESTABLISH THEIR OWN COUNTRY BY REVOLTING AGAINST THE HAPSBURG MONARCHY IN 1848. THE REBELLION WAS VIOLENTLY CRUSHED AND OPPRESSION FOLLOWED.
MANY CZECH PATRIOTS LOOKED TOWARD AMERICA FOR FREEDOM AND OPPORTUNITY. SIXTEEN CZECH FAMILIES LEFT HAMBURG, GERMANY IN 1852 AND SPENT SEVENTEEN MISERABLE WEEKS AT SEA ON A LEAKY, DIRTY SHIP WITH ONLY RAW FOOD TO EAT. WHEN THEY ARRIVED AT GALVESTON, THEY BECAME THE FIRST GROUP OF CZECH IMMIGRANTS TO REACH TEXAS.

SECOND OF TWO PARTS

THE CZECH-TEXANS

AFTER ARRIVING AT GALVESTON IN 1852 MANY OF THE FIRST CZECHS IN TEXAS WENT BY OX CART TO THE AREA BETWEEN CAT SPRING & NEW ULM IN AUSTIN COUNTY. THIS BECAME KNOWN AS THE **NEW BREMEN** SETTLEMENT, ONE OF THE FIRST CZECH CENTERS IN TEXAS.

AN INHERENT TALENT FOR FARMING LED THE CZECHS TO SETTLE ON THE RICHEST SOIL IN TEXAS FROM DENTON TO BROWNSVILLE. OVER 90 % OF THE CZECH-TEXANS LIVE IN 32 CONTIGUOUS COUNTIES INCLUDING LAVACA, BURLESON, WILLIAMSON, WHARTON, VICTORIA, MCLENNAN, FORT BEND AND BELL. **FAYETTEVILLE** IN EASTERN FAYETTE COUNTY IS OFTEN CALLED "THE CRADLE OF CZECH SETTLEMENT IN TEXAS."

Fort Lancaster,
BUILT IN 1855 BY THE U.S. ARMY, WAS PART OF A SERIES OF OUTPOSTS THAT PROTECTED TRAVELERS AND MAIL ON THE "LOWER" OVERLAND ROUTE FROM SAN ANTONIO TO SAN DIEGO.
DURING THE CIVIL WAR THE FORT WAS OCCUPIED BY THE 2nd TEXAS CAVALRY, THEN ABANDONED IN 1861.
AFTER BRIEFLY BEING USED AS A BIVOUAC SITE FOR U.S. TROOPS IN 1867 & '71 THE FORT FELL TO RUIN. TODAY FORT LANCASTER IS A STATE HISTORIC SITE NEAR THE PECOS RIVER IN CROCKETT COUNTY.

CAMP FORD NEAR **TYLER** WAS BUILT IN 1862 BY COL. "RIP" FORD AS A TRAINING BASE FOR CONFEDERATE RECRUITS BUT BECAME THE LARGEST **PRISONER** OF WAR **CAMP** WEST OF THE MISSISSIPPI DURING THE CIVIL WAR. AT ONE TIME NEARLY 6000 YANKEE SOLDIERS FROM OVER 100 REGIMENTS AND SAILORS FROM GUNBOATS LIVED HERE IN CROWDED, PARTLY FINISHED, DARK AND DIRTY SHANTIES CALLED

"SHEBANGS."

ACCORDING TO ONE HISTORICAL WRITER, ONE OF THESE PRISONERS MUST HAVE SERVED UNDER GENERAL DOUBLEDAY, BECAUSE HE INTRODUCED THE GAME OF **BASEBALL** TO TEXAS.

CAMP FORD CONTINUED AS A PRISON CAMP UNTIL MAY, 1865. UNION RECONSTRUCTION FORCES DESTROYED IT. TYLER CITIZENS PURCHASED THE SITE (ON U.S. RT. 271) AND PLACED A GRANITE MARKER THERE.

Andrew Jackson Potter

WAS BORN APRIL, 1830 IN MISSOURI AND ORPHANED BY THE AGE OF TEN.

HE EARNED HIS KEEP BY JOCKEYING RACE-HORSES & PLAYING CARDS. HIS "FORMAL" EDUCATION CAME FROM GAMBLERS AND GUNMEN.

AT AGE SIXTEEN HE JOINED THE ARMY AND SERVED IN THE MEXICAN WAR AS A SCOUT, A HOSPITAL WAGON NURSE AND AN OX-TEAM DRIVER.

IN 1852 POTTER MOVED TO SAN ANTONIO, MARRIED EMILY GUIN, DROVE A FREIGHT WAGON AND GOT INTO A LOT OF BARROOM BRAWLS.

AFTER ATTENDING A CAMP MEETING IN 1856 HE BEGAN TO STUDY THE BIBLE AND BY 1859 WAS ORDAINED A **METHODIST MINISTER.**

FORMER RACING-JOCKEY, GAMBLER, SALOON-BRAWLER-TURNED-METHODIST MINISTER ANDREW JACKSON POTTER JOINED THE 32nd TEXAS CAVALRY AS CHAPLAIN DURING THE CIVIL WAR. ONE DAY HE READ AN UNCOMPLIMENTARY ARTICLE ABOUT HIS REGIMENT IN A BROWNSVILLE PAPER, SO HE CALLED ON THE EDITOR...
FROM THEN ON HE WAS KNOWN AS
the Fighting Parson.
AFTER THE WAR REV. POTTER TRAVELED THROUGHOUT WEST TEXAS WITH HIS BIBLE AND GUNS EVER READY. SINCE CHURCHES WERE SCARCE ON THE FRONTIER HE OFTEN "SET UP SHOP" IN SALOONS.
IN 1883 HE FINALLY SETTLED WITH HIS WIFE AND 14 CHILDREN IN SAN ANGELO.

PRIOR TO THE 1880'S MOST PLACES ON THE NORTHERN FRONTIER RELIED ON THE TEXAS RANGERS TO MAINTAIN LAW AND ORDER.

COPE WILLINGHAM

BROUGHT THE LAW TO **OLDHAM COUNTY** WHEN HE BECAME ITS **FIRST SHERIFF** IN 1880. ONE DAY FRED LEIGH AND FOUR OF HIS GUN-SLINGING BUDDIES VISITED A CROSSROADS SALOON. COPE GREETED THEM: "HOWDY, BOYS...I MUST NOT ONLY RELIEVE YOU OF YOUR ARTILLERY, BUT I'M TAKIN' YOU TO THE JUSTICE OF THE PEACE FOR CARRYIN' WEAPONS."

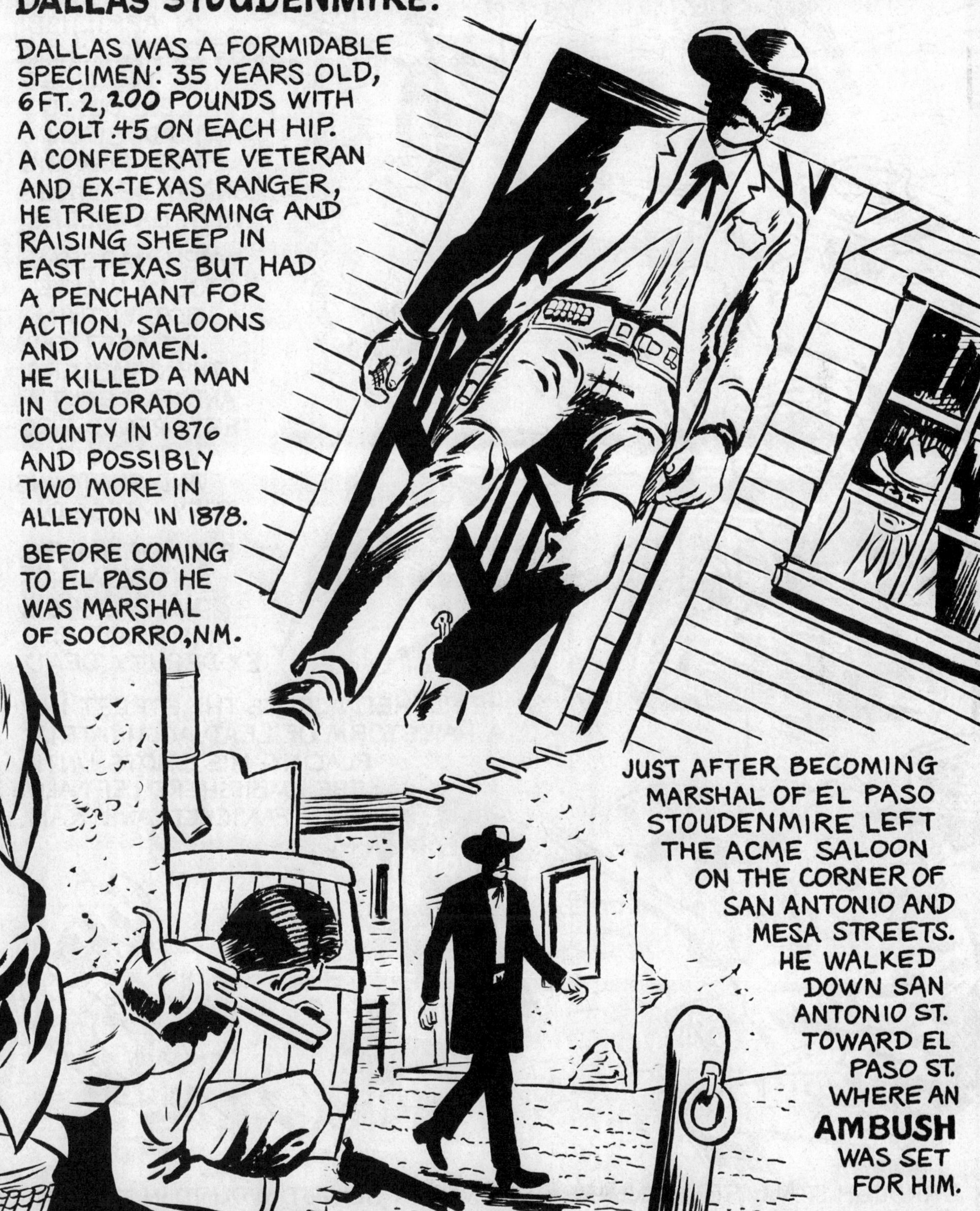
THE MARSHAL
FIRST OF THREE PARTS
THINGS HAD GOTTEN OUT OF HAND IN EL PASO IN 1881; THE LOCAL CONSTABULARY WAS INCAPABLE OF KEEPING THE PEACE. DOC CUMMINGS, OWNER OF THE GLOBE RESTAURANT, SUMMONED HIS BROTHER-IN-LAW DALLAS STOUDENMIRE.
DALLAS WAS A FORMIDABLE SPECIMEN: 35 YEARS OLD, 6 FT. 2, 200 POUNDS WITH A COLT .45 ON EACH HIP. A CONFEDERATE VETERAN AND EX-TEXAS RANGER, HE TRIED FARMING AND RAISING SHEEP IN EAST TEXAS BUT HAD A PENCHANT FOR ACTION, SALOONS AND WOMEN. HE KILLED A MAN IN COLORADO COUNTY IN 1876 AND POSSIBLY TWO MORE IN ALLEYTON IN 1878.
BEFORE COMING TO EL PASO HE WAS MARSHAL OF SOCORRO, NM.
JUST AFTER BECOMING MARSHAL OF EL PASO STOUDENMIRE LEFT THE ACME SALOON ON THE CORNER OF SAN ANTONIO AND MESA STREETS. HE WALKED DOWN SAN ANTONIO ST. TOWARD EL PASO ST. WHERE AN AMBUSH WAS SET FOR HIM.

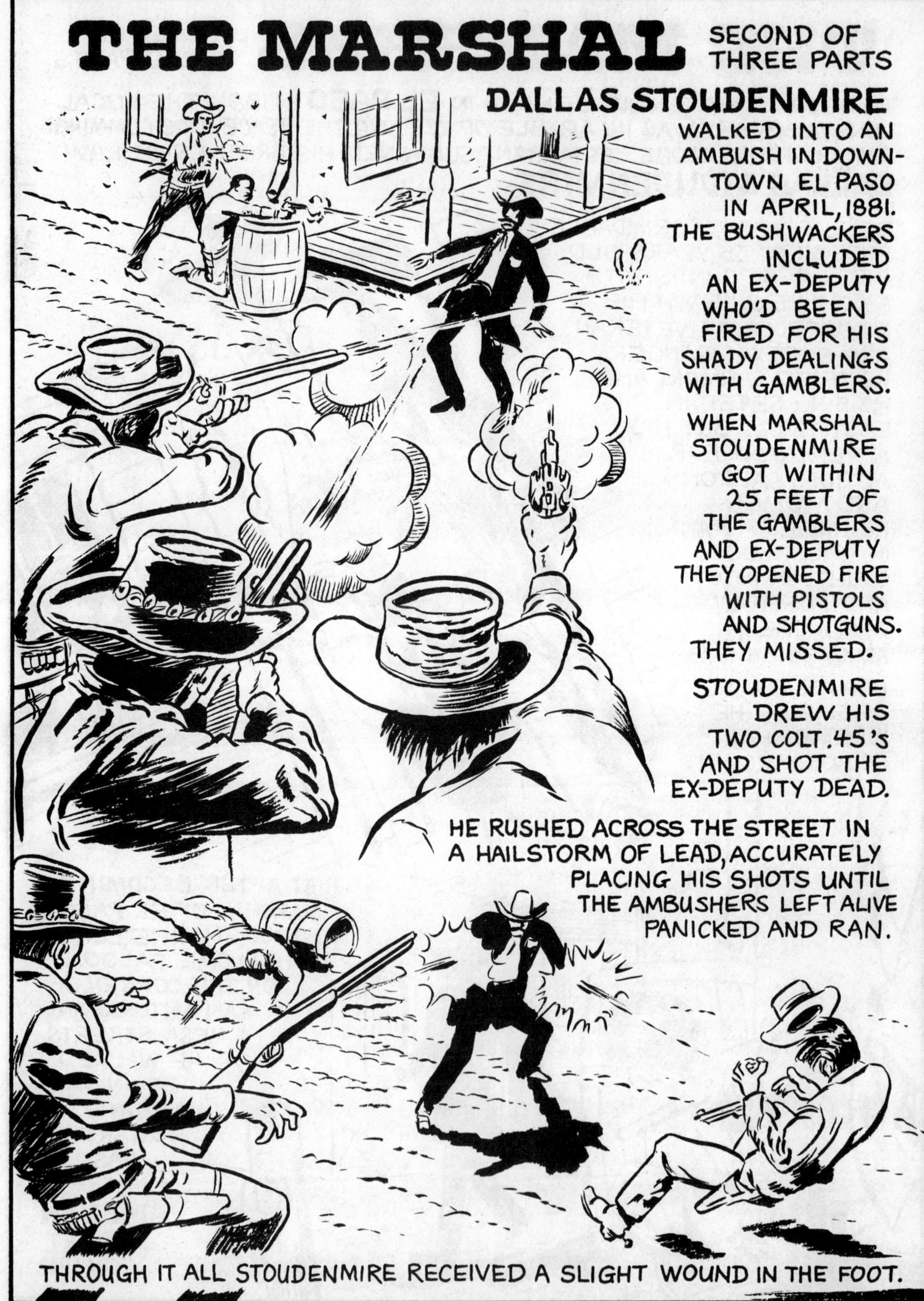
THE MARSHAL
SECOND OF THREE PARTS
DALLAS STOUDENMIRE WALKED INTO AN AMBUSH IN DOWN-TOWN EL PASO IN APRIL, 1881. THE BUSHWACKERS INCLUDED AN EX-DEPUTY WHO'D BEEN FIRED FOR HIS SHADY DEALINGS WITH GAMBLERS.
WHEN MARSHAL STOUDENMIRE GOT WITHIN 25 FEET OF THE GAMBLERS AND EX-DEPUTY THEY OPENED FIRE WITH PISTOLS AND SHOTGUNS. THEY MISSED.
STOUDENMIRE DREW HIS TWO COLT .45's AND SHOT THE EX-DEPUTY DEAD.
HE RUSHED ACROSS THE STREET IN A HAILSTORM OF LEAD, ACCURATELY PLACING HIS SHOTS UNTIL THE AMBUSHERS LEFT ALIVE PANICKED AND RAN.
THROUGH IT ALL STOUDENMIRE RECEIVED A SLIGHT WOUND IN THE FOOT.

THE MARSHAL

LAST OF THREE PARTS

A FEUD STARTED IN EL PASO IN THE SPRING OF 1881 AFTER AN ATTEMPT TO BUSHWACK THE NEW MARSHAL, DALLAS STOUDENMIRE, FAILED. HIS BROTHER-IN-LAW, DOC CUMMINGS TRIED TO AVENGE THE ATTEMPTED ASSASSINATION BUT WAS SHOT.

FINALLY, IN APRIL, 1882, ALL PARTIES IN THE FEUD-MARSHAL STOUDENMIRE AND THE LOCAL SPORTING CROWD-SIGNED A TREATY WHICH SAID IN PART "LET BYGONES BE BYGONES."

IT WAS SIGNED BY STOUDENMIRE AND BROTHERS JIM, FRANK AND DR. G.F. MANNING. A SHORT TIME LATER JIM MANNING, WHO BOASTED OF KILLING CUMMINGS, SHOT THE MARSHAL TO DEATH DURING AN ARGUMENT OVER WHETHER THE TREATY HAD BEEN BROKEN.

SARAH BURGETT WAS AN ENTERPRISING WOMAN WHO RAN EATING PLACES AND BORDELLOS FROM FLORIDA TO ARIZONA IN THE MID 1800'S. HER IMPRESSIVE FIGURE, WELL OVER 6 FT. TALL, PROMPTED FOLKS TO CALL HER

THE GREAT WESTERN.

DURING THE MEXICAN WAR SHE RAN A COMBINATION RESTAURANT-BROTHEL FOR AMERICAN GI'S AT SALTILLO.

WHEN FIGHTING ERUPTED NEARBY SHE TURNED HER "HOUSE" INTO A HOSPITAL AND CARRIED WOUNDED MEN OFF THE BATTLEFIELD WHILE FIRING THEIR RIFLES AT THE ENEMY.

AFTER THE WAR, IN 1849, SHE BECAME THE FIRST MADAM-OF-RECORD IN **EL PASO** WHEN SHE ERECTED A RESTAURANT-HOTEL-BORDELLO THERE.

THE GREAT WESTERN DIED IN YUMA, AZ. IN 1866 AND WAS BURIED WITH FULL MILITARY HONORS.

WHILE JOHN F. GLIDDEN OF ILLINOIS IS CREDITED WITH THE
first barbed wire patent
IN 1874, JOHN GRINNINGER REPORTEDLY INVENTED BARBED WIRE IN AN AUSTIN FOUNDRY WHERE HE WORKED IN 1857. HE USED IT TO FENCE IN HIS SMALL GARDEN ON WALLER CREEK.
MR. GLIDDEN HIRED H.B. SANBORN TO SELL HIS WIRE. SANBORN'S FIRST SALE WAS FOR TWO REELS TO A MERCHANT IN GAINESVILLE. SHORTLY AFTERWARDS A HARDWARE STORE IN AUSTIN BOUGHT A CARLOAD.
A TOWN IN GRAYSON COUNTY, WHERE HE OWNED A RANCH, IS NAMED AFTER SANBORN.

BORN IN SABINE COUNTY ON FEBRUARY 9, 1837,

Christopher Columbus Slaughter

LEARNED THE CATTLE BUSINESS AT THE AGE OF 12 FROM HIS FATHER, GEORGE, ON THE PATROON BAYOU-SABINE RIVER DIVIDE. HIS FAMILY MOVED TO FREESTONE COUNTY IN 1852. AT AGE 17, C.C. BECAME AN EXPERT AT TAKING CATTLE ACROSS THE TRINITY RIVER.

AT THIS TIME C.C. STARTED TO BECOME ONE OF AMERICA'S SHREWDEST BUSINESSMEN. BUYING LUMBER IN ANDERSON COUNTY HE SOLD IT TO SETTLERS IN DALLAS, THEN BOUGHT WHEAT IN COLLIN COUNTY, GROUND IT INTO FLOUR AND SOLD IT IN MAGNOLIA. THIS ALL TOOK THREE MONTHS AND HE RETURNED HOME WITH A PROFIT OF $520.

WITH THIS HE BOUGHT HIS UNCLE'S INTEREST (ABOUT 70 HEAD) IN THE SMALL SLAUGHTER HERD OF CATTLE. THUS BEGAN AN EMPIRE!

BY 1865 THE SLAUGHTER HERD NUMBERED 1500 HEAD AND WAS MOVED TO A LARGER RANGE IN PALO PINTO COUNTY. (BEFORE HIS 20th BIRTHDAY C.C. SLAUGHTER SOLD 300 BEEVES TO A JEFFERSON PACKERY AT $35 A HEAD IN GOLD, A HITHERTO UNHEARD OF PRICE FOR TEXAS STEERS.)

Christopher Columbus Slaughter

PIONEERED THE CROSS-BREEDING AND IMPROVEMENT OF TEXAS LONGHORNS WHILE EXPANDING HIS LAND HOLDINGS UNTIL HE OWNED OVER A MILLION ACRES. HE WAS THE LARGEST INDIVIDUAL LAND OWNER AND TAXPAYER IN TEXAS BY 1887. A NOTORIOUS NICKEL-NURSER, C.C. ADMITTED IN HIS LATER YEARS ALMOST GRUDGINGLY THAT...

A COWBOY WHO MADE IT UP THE LADDER TO **CATTLE BARON** WAS

BORN MARCH 5, 1836 IN MACOUPIN COUNTY, ILLINOIS, HE WAS BROUGHT TO MILAM COUNTY, TX. BY HIS MOTHER AND STEP-FATHER IN 1846. A YEAR LATER THEY MOVED TO **PALO PINTO** COUNTY WHERE CHARLIE WORKED WITH HIS STEP-BROTHER AS A COWBOY. THEY WERE PAID IN CATTLE AND BY 1860 OWNED 180 HEAD.

DURING THE CIVIL WAR HE WAS A CONFEDERATE SCOUT AND TEXAS RANGER.

HE TEAMED UP WITH OLIVER LOVING TO SEEK BETTER MARKETS FOR THEIR BEEF THAN WERE OFFERED IN TEXAS DURING RECONSTRUCTION. THEY BLAZED THE GOODNIGHT-LOVING TRAIL FROM FORT BELKNAP, TX. TO FORT SUMNER, NEW MEXICO.

CHARLIE FAILED AT RANCHING IN COLORADO IN 1875, THEN MOVED TO THE PALO DURO CANYON IN THE TEXAS PANHANDLE. EVENTUALLY HE PRESIDED OVER A HERD OF OVER 100,000 HEAD, SELLING 30,000 ANIMALS IN AN AVERAGE SEASON FOR A GROSS INCOME OF ABOUT $500,000.

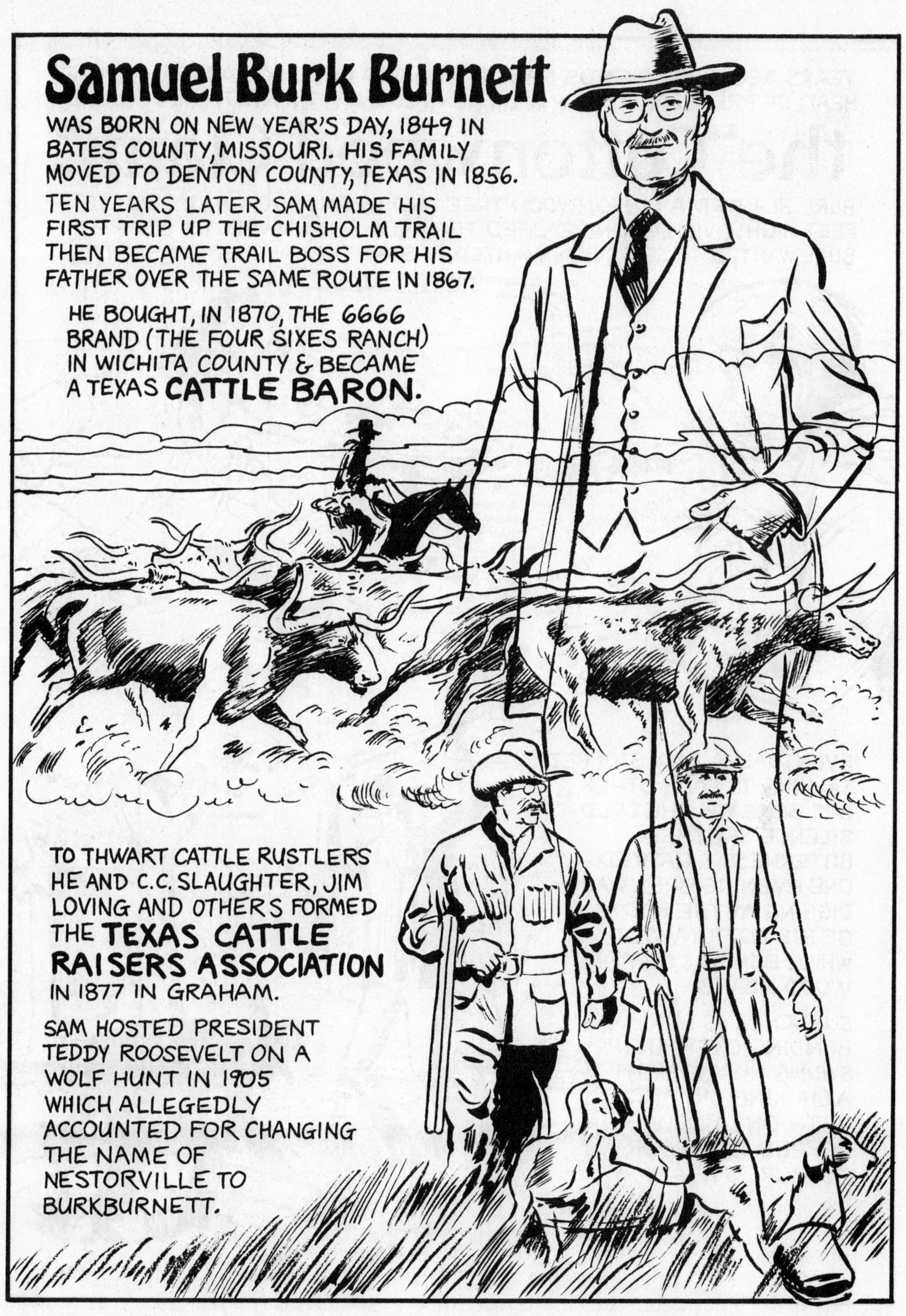
Samuel Burk Burnett
WAS BORN ON NEW YEAR'S DAY, 1849 IN BATES COUNTY, MISSOURI. HIS FAMILY MOVED TO DENTON COUNTY, TEXAS IN 1856.
TEN YEARS LATER SAM MADE HIS FIRST TRIP UP THE CHISHOLM TRAIL THEN BECAME TRAIL BOSS FOR HIS FATHER OVER THE SAME ROUTE IN 1867.
HE BOUGHT, IN 1870, THE 6666 BRAND (THE FOUR SIXES RANCH) IN WICHITA COUNTY & BECAME A TEXAS CATTLE BARON.
TO THWART CATTLE RUSTLERS HE AND C.C. SLAUGHTER, JIM LOVING AND OTHERS FORMED THE TEXAS CATTLE RAISERS ASSOCIATION IN 1877 IN GRAHAM.
SAM HOSTED PRESIDENT TEDDY ROOSEVELT ON A WOLF HUNT IN 1905 WHICH ALLEGEDLY ACCOUNTED FOR CHANGING THE NAME OF NESTORVILLE TO BURKBURNETT.

YEARS AGO TWO FRIENDS NAMED BEN AND BURL SQUATTED AT THE HEAD OF PRESSLAR'S DRAW IN DICKENS COUNTY ON WHAT THEY CALLED
the "Cottonwood Claim."
BURL PLANTED A COTTONWOOD TREE AND WHEN IT REACHED TWELVE FEET HIGH CIVILIZATION REACHED THE AREA & LAND VALUES SOARED. BURL WANTED TO SELL; BEN WANTED TO STAY. THEY ARGUED CONSTANTLY.
EVENTUALLY THEY STOPPED TALKING TO EACH OTHER, BUT BENEATH THE COLD SILENCE SEETHED BITTERNESS & HATRED. ONE EVENING BURL WAS DIGGING AT THE ROOTS OF HIS COTTONWOOD WHILE BEN WAS CHOPPING WOOD NEARBY.
SUDDENLY, AS BURL WAS BENDING OVER, BEN SWUNG HIS AXE WITH A CHOKING CRY AND WITH ONE BLOW LOPPED OFF POOR OL' BURL'S HEAD.

A DISPUTE OVER SELLING THEIR "**COTTONWOOD CLAIM**" RESULTED IN BEN DECAPITATING HIS PARTNER, BURL. A FEW MONTHS LATER BEN WENT CRAZY, CONVINCED HE WAS BEING HAUNTED BY THE GHOST OF

THE HEADLESS SQUATTER

THUS HOUNDED, HE **CONFESSED** HIS CRIME TO THE SHERIFF.

BUT BEN HAD ALREADY ACQUIRED THE REPUTATION OF BEING "CRACKED", SO NOBODY PAID ANY ATTENTION TO HIM. ONE DAY A RIDER FOUND THE BLOATED BODY OF BEN HANGING FROM THE COTTONWOOD TREE THAT BURL PLANTED.

FOLKS IN THE AREA SAY THAT AT NIGHT PHANTOMS CAN STILL BE SEEN CROSSING THE OLD "KENZIE" TRAIL AT PRESSLAR'S DRAW IN DICKENS COUNTY... AND SOME HAVE HEARD THE CRY "O-O-O-O BEN" COMING FROM THE OLD COTTONWOOD TREE.

IT DOESN'T TAKE MUCH—A WIND-BLOWN HAT, A SNEEZE, A SUDDEN YELL OR LAUGH—TO START A STAMPEDE. NORTHWEST BETWEEN CROSBYTON AND SPUR, AT THE CAP ROCK CLIFFS, IS A PLACE CALLED

Stampede Mesa.

THE MESA HAD WATER AND GOOD GRASS FOR A NIGHT CAMP ON A TRAIL DRIVE BUT IT ALSO SLOPED UPWARD TO AN ABRUPT END IN HUNDRED FOOT CLIFFS. ONE DAY IN THE 1880'S A DROVER CAMPED THERE WITH A THOUSAND HEAD. DURING THE NIGHT THE HERD STAMPEDED. HUNDREDS OF LONGHORNS AND TWO COWBOYS WENT OVER THE CLIFFS.

TRAIL BOSSES AVOIDED *STAMPEDE MESA* AFTER THAT. TODAY SOME FOLKS CLAIM YOU CAN SEE GHOST RIDERS AND CATTLE STAMPEDING OFF THOSE CLIFFS.

Saluting the Centennial of Edwards County

ORGANIZED 1883 IT HAS MORE **ANGORA GOATS** THAN PEOPLE. THESE ANIMALS PRODUCE MORE MOHAIR FOR RUGS, CLOTHING & DRAPERIES THAN ANY OTHER GOATS IN THE U.S.

THE **DEVIL'S SINKHOLE** NEAR ROCKSPRINGS IS THE LARGEST SINKHOLE IN THE COUNTRY. FORMED MILLIONS OF YEARS AGO, IT HAS A 60-FT. DIAMETER ENTRANCE, AND MANY UNEXPLORED ROOMS & TUNNELS. THE MAIN CHAMBER PLUNGES MORE THAN 300 FEET INTO WATER.

Saluting the Centennial of Scurry County
IN 1877 W. H. "PETE" SNYDER HAULED LUMBER AND MERCHANDISE TO THE COUNTY, BUILT A TRADING POST AND BEGAN DEALING WITH BUFFALO HUNTERS. HE LAID OUT A TOWN IN 1882 AND NAMED IT AFTER HIMSELF. WHEN SCURRY COUNTY WAS ORGANIZED ON JUNE 28, 1884 SNYDER BECAME THE COUNTY SEAT.
E.I. "TOMMY" THOMPSON DRILLED THE FIRST SUCCESSFUL OIL WELL IN 1923. TODAY SCURRY COUNTY IS AMERICA'S NO. 1 OIL PRODUCING COUNTY, ANNUALLY PUMPING ABOUT 30 MILLION BARRELS FROM 49 DESIGNATED FIELDS. THIS GOLD PUMP JACK COMMEMORATES THE SITE THAT PRODUCED SCURRY'S BILLIONTH BARREL.
SACROC UNIT
TRACT 51
WELL NO. 4
Billionth Barrel
OCT. 1973
SCURRY COUNTY, TEX

Saluting the Centennial of Zavala County

A SPANISH EXPEDITION UNDER DOMINGO TERAN DE LOS RIOS EXPLORED THE ZAVALA COUNTY AREA IN 1691. THE OLD SAN ANTONIO ROAD BETWEEN EAGLE PASS & SAN ANTONIO WENT ACROSS THE COUNTY & WAS USED BY ALMOST ALL THE EXPLORERS & TRAVELERS IN THE 18th CENTURY.

CREATED FROM UVALDE & MAVERICK COUNTIES IN 1858, THE COUNTY WAS NAMED FOR TEXAS COLONIST LORENZO DE ZAVALA. NOT UNTIL FEB. 25th, 1884 DID ENOUGH FOLKS LIVE THERE TO PERMIT IT TO BE ORGANIZED. BATESVILLE WAS THE COUNTY SEAT UNTIL IT WAS MOVED TO CRYSTAL CITY IN 1928.

DURING THE CIVIL WAR A CONFEDERATE REGIMENT UNDER COL. JAMES M. NORRIS OCCUPIED CAMP NUECES NEAR LA PRYOR. THEIR JOB WAS TO SEE THAT COTTON GOT TO MEXICO WHILE MUNITIONS, MEDICINE AND SUPPLIES GOT TO THE CONFEDERACY. IT HAD NO FAMOUS BATTLES; IT DID HAVE PLENTY OF HARDSHIPS.

First of two Parts
Old Rip
WHEN THE CORNER-STONE OF THE EASTLAND COURTHOUSE WAS BEING DEDICATED JUSTICE OF THE PEACE EARNEST WOOD NOTICED THAT HIS SON WAS PLAYING WITH A HORNED TOAD.
THIS GAVE HIM THE IDEA TO PUT THE TOAD IN THE CORNERSTONE
1897
THE COURTHOUSE WAS TO BE TORN DOWN IN 1928 TO MAKE WAY FOR A NEW ONE. A HUGE CROWD GATHERED TO WATCH JUDGE PRITCHARD REMOVE THE CONTENTS OF THE CORNERSTONE. EUGENE DAY, AN OIL MAN, LIFTED OUT "OLD RIP," AND HANDED IT TO REV. SINGLETON WHO HANDED IT TO THE JUDGE.
1897
SUDDENLY "OLD RIP" TWITCHED TO LIFE!

Second of two parts
Old Rip
AFTER A 31-YEAR "NAP" IN THE CORNERSTONE OF THE EASTLAND COURTHOUSE THE HORNED TOAD, OLD RIP, EMERGED **ALIVE** AND AN INSTANT **CELEBRITY.**
OLD RIP WAS EXHIBITED ALL OVER THE U.S. & EVEN PAID A VISIT TO PRES. CALVIN COOLIDGE.
PRESIDENT
ON SATURDAY, JANUARY 19, 1929 OLD RIP DIED OF **PNEUMONIA.** HIS BODY WAS EMBALMED AND CAN BE SEEN DAY AND NIGHT IN A PLUSH-LINED COFFIN CUSTOM-MADE BY THE ABILENE CASKET COMPANY IN THE **LOBBY** OF THE NEW **EASTLAND** COUNTY COURTHOUSE.

FIRST OF THREE PARTS

THE CISCO SANTA

'TWAS THE DAY BEFORE CHRISTMAS, 1927 WHEN A MAN IN SANTA CLAUS DUDS WALKED INTO THE FIRST NATIONAL BANK AT CISCO FOLLOWED BY HIS THREE "HELPERS" AND SOME CHILDREN. AT THE TELLER'S WINDOW SANTA DID NOT SAY "HO-HO-HO." HE SAID "**STICK 'EM UP!**"

BY THE TIME THE DESPERADOES HAD COLLECTED THE MONEY AN ALARM BROUGHT THE POLICE TO THE SCENE.

A GUNFIGHT ENSUED IN WHICH TWO COPS, SEVERAL CITIZENS AND ONE ROBBER WERE WOUNDED.

AS THEY FLED "SANTA" AND HIS HOODLUMS SNATCHED TWO LITTLE GIRLS AND TOOK THEM ALONG AS **HOSTAGES.**

SECOND OF THREE PARTS

THE CISCO SANTA

A THIEF DISGUISED AS SANTA CLAUS AND HIS THREE "HELPERS" ROBBED THE BANK IN CISCO ON CHRISTMAS EVE, 1927, ESCAPED DURING A SHOOT-OUT AND TOOK TWO KIDS AS HOSTAGES. A FEW BLOCKS FROM THE BANK THEY TRIED TO CHANGE CARS BUT THE SECOND CAR WOULD NOT START.

THE POSSE WAS CLOSING IN SO THE CROOKS ABANDONED THE 2nd CAR WITH THE $12,000 LOOT ALONG WITH THEIR WOUNDED COHORT. THEY TOOK OFF IN THE FIRST CAR, TAKING THE KIDS WITH THEM. BY NIGHTFALL THE POLICE FOUND THAT CAR AND THE CHILDREN UNHARMED. THE WOUNDED GUNMAN DIED ON CHRISTMAS DAY.

LAST OF THREE PARTS

THE CISCO SANTA

A MAN DRESSED UP AS SANTA CLAUS WITH THREE HELPERS ROBBED $12,000 FROM A BANK IN CISCO ON CHRISTMAS EVE, 1927. DURING THEIR ESCAPE ONE WAS KILLED.

ON DEC. 27 THE POLICE CAUGHT UP WITH "SANTA" IN SOUTH BEND, 40 MILES NORTH OF CISCO ON RT. 67. ARMED WITH FOUR GERMAN LUGERS, TWO AUTOMATIC PISTOLS, A DOUBLE BARREL SHOTGUN AND A BOWIE KNIFE "SANTA" HELD OFF THE COPS UNTIL HE WAS WOUNDED & CAPTURED.

THE TWO REMAINING BANDITS GOT AWAY AND MADE IT ABOUT TEN MILES FURTHER NORTH. FINALLY, SICK FROM EXPOSURE AND WOUNDS RECEIVED IN THE PREVIOUS GUN BATTLE, THEY SURRENDERED TO POLICE IN GRAHAM ON DECEMBER 30th. FOR MANY CHRISTMASES THEREAFTER "SANTA & HIS HELPERS" DECKED THE HALLS OF THE PENITENTIARY.

IN 1849 HEINRICH L. KREISCHE, A GERMAN IMMIGRANT AND STONE MASON, BOUGHT 172 ACRES OF HILLY LAND OVERLOOKING THE COLORADO RIVER JUST SOUTH OF LA GRANGE. HERE HE BUILT A HUGE HOME, SMOKEHOUSE, BARN AND A COMPLEX THREE-STORIED BUILDING THAT SOME TIME DURING THE 1860'S BECAME ONE OF THE FIRST OF ITS KIND IN TEXAS:
the Kreische Brewery.
KREISCHE'S BEER WET THE WHISTLES OF IMBIBERS AT A BEER GARDEN ON HIS ESTATE AND A SALOON IN LA GRANGE.
THE BREWERY BECAME THE THIRD LARGEST IN TEXAS, BUT AFTER KREISCHE DIED IN 1882 IT FOLDED, THEN FELL TO RUIN.
THE STATE ACQUIRED THE SITE IN 1977 AND BEGAN PRESERVATION WORK.
TODAY TEXAS IS PROBABLY THE ONLY STATE THAT HONORS AN OLD BREWERY AS A STATE HISTORIC SITE.

FIRST OF FOUR PARTS
The Hatchet Lady
TEN YEARS AFTER HER HUSBAND DIED OF ALCOHOLISM CARRY GLOYD MARRIED DAVID NATION, AN ATTORNEY & PREACHER. THEY BOUGHT A FARM IN BRAZORIA COUNTY IN 1879 BUT ALMOST STARVED TO DEATH BECAUSE NEITHER KNEW ANYTHING ABOUT FARMING. WHEN DAVID FAILED TO GET A JOB, CARRY, WITH $3.50 CAPITAL RENTED AND OPERATED THE OLD COLUMBIA HOTEL.
HER EARNINGS WERE MEAGER. DAVID CONTRIBUTED LITTLE BUT DRANK MUCH. HER DAUGHTER HAD MENTAL PROBLEMS ALL HER LIFE. CARRY DEALT WITH THESE TROUBLES BY BECOMING FANATICALLY RELIGIOUS AND AN OUTSPOKEN OPPONENT OF BOOZE, BARS & BROTHERHOOD LODGES.
SHE RAN A HOTEL IN RICHMOND, TX. IN 1881 BUT MOST PEOPLE AVOIDED HER. NINE YEARS LATER THE NATIONS MOVED TO KANSAS.

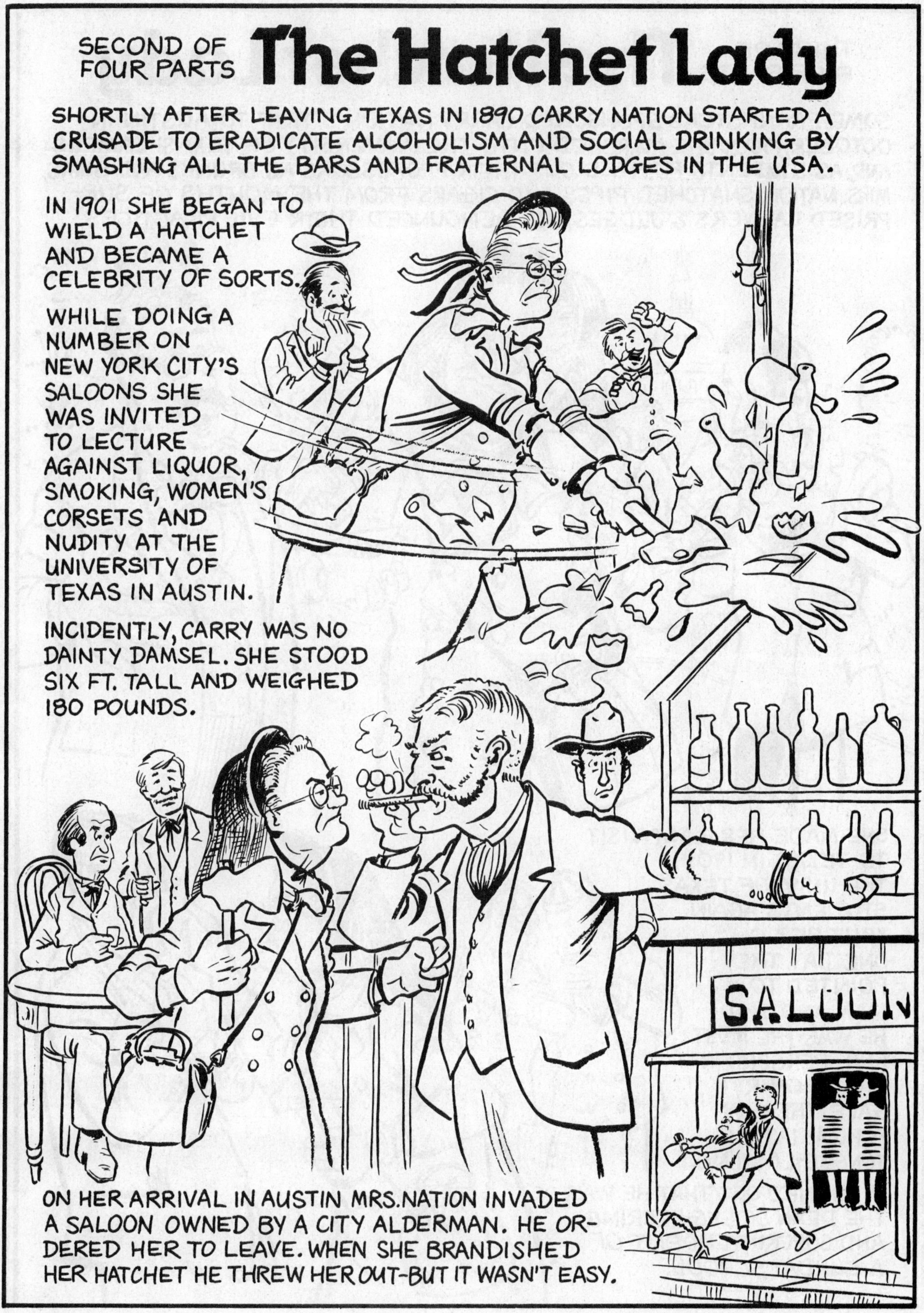

SECOND OF FOUR PARTS

The Hatchet Lady

SHORTLY AFTER LEAVING TEXAS IN 1890 CARRY NATION STARTED A CRUSADE TO ERADICATE ALCOHOLISM AND SOCIAL DRINKING BY SMASHING ALL THE BARS AND FRATERNAL LODGES IN THE USA.

IN 1901 SHE BEGAN TO WIELD A HATCHET AND BECAME A CELEBRITY OF SORTS.

WHILE DOING A NUMBER ON NEW YORK CITY'S SALOONS SHE WAS INVITED TO LECTURE AGAINST LIQUOR, SMOKING, WOMEN'S CORSETS AND NUDITY AT THE UNIVERSITY OF TEXAS IN AUSTIN.

INCIDENTLY, CARRY WAS NO DAINTY DAMSEL. SHE STOOD SIX FT. TALL AND WEIGHED 180 POUNDS.

SALOON

ON HER ARRIVAL IN AUSTIN MRS. NATION INVADED A SALOON OWNED BY A CITY ALDERMAN. HE ORDERED HER TO LEAVE. WHEN SHE BRANDISHED HER HATCHET HE THREW HER OUT-BUT IT WASN'T EASY.

THIRD OF FOUR PARTS

The Hatchet Lady

SOME PRANKSTERS SPONSORED CARRY NATION'S TRIP TO AUSTIN IN OCTOBER, 1902. SHE MARCHED ONTO THE UNIVERSITY OF TEXAS' CAMPUS AND, AS STUDENTS POINTED OUT THEIR PROFESSORS AS DRUNKS AND BUMS, MRS. NATION SNATCHED PIPES AND CIGARS FROM THE MOUTHS OF SURPRISED LAWYERS & JUDGES AND DENOUNCED THEIR EVIL PRACTICES.

SHE MADE HER LAST VISIT TO TEXAS IN 1904. THE UNIV. OF TEXAS STUDENTS AGAIN "PUT HER ON." ONE DAY THEY POINTED TO A MAN AND SAID HE WAS THE MOST EVIL PERSON ON EARTH. CARRY GAVE THE GUY A HUMILIATING TONGUE-LASHING.

IT TURNED OUT THAT HE WAS THE DEAN OF ENGINEERING AND SUPERINTENDENT OF A SUNDAY SCHOOL.

LAST OF FOUR PARTS

The Hatchet Lady

CARRY NATION STARTED HER CRUSADE AGAINST SMOKING, DRINKING AND IMMORALITY IN TEXAS IN THE LATE 1880's AND CARRIED IT ACROSS THE COUNTRY BY SMASHING SALOONS. SHE WAS JAILED IN 25 STATES AND PAID FOR HER LEGAL FEES BY SELLING TOY HATCHETS. DURING HER RAIDS SHE DID SOME AMAZING FEATS OF STRENGTH LIKE HURLING CASH REGISTERS ACROSS ROOMS AND TEARING ICEBOX DOORS OFF THEIR HINGES.

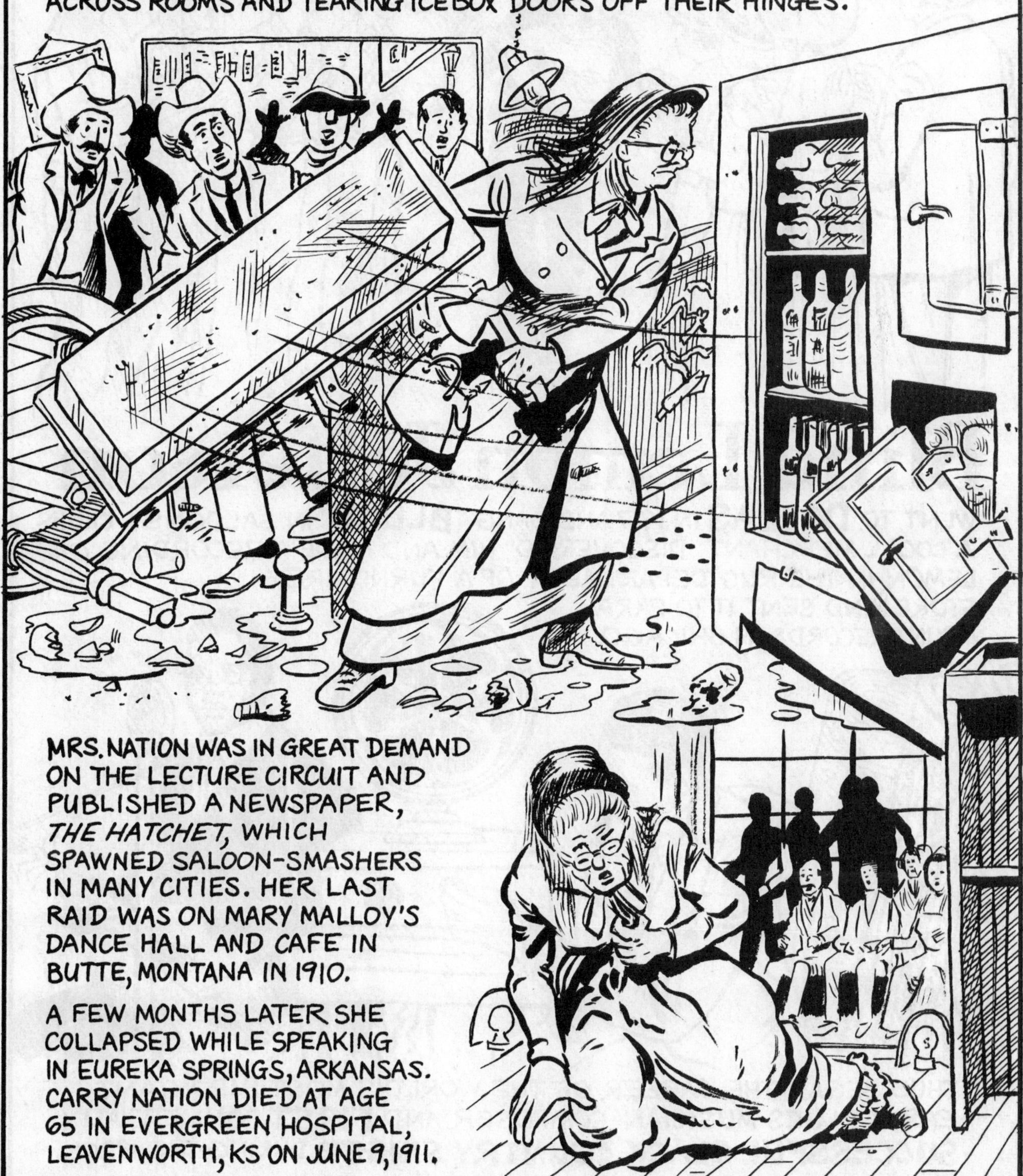

A BABY WAS BORN BLIND ON A FARM OUTSIDE **COUCHMAN** IN 1897. AS A TEENAGER THE ONLY WAY HE COULD EARN MONEY WAS BY **SINGING.** SO HE'D WALK TO WORTHAM AND SING ON STREET CORNERS. BY THE TIME HE WAS TWENTY HE WAS SINGING AT PARTIES AND DANCES THROUGHOUT **FREESTONE COUNTY.**

Blind Lemon Jefferson

WENT TO **DALLAS** IN 1917 AND SANG **"BLUES"** IN SALOONS & CLUBS. A LOCAL MERCHANT "DISCOVERED" HIM AND MADE A RECORDING OF LEMON IN THE RUG DEPARTMENT OF A FURNITURE STORE AND SENT IT TO PARAMOUNT RECORDS IN CHICAGO.

THUS BEGAN THE CAREER OF THE WORLD'S MOST IMPORTANT EARLY BLUES MUSICIAN-COMPOSER AND **FIRST** COMMERCIALLY **SUCCESSFUL BLACK COUNTRY SINGER** DURING THE 1920'S.

HIS RELAXED TROMBONE STYLING AND VOICE THAT RANGED BETWEEN THE RASP OF LOUIS ARMSTRONG & SMOOTHNESS OF BING CROSBY MADE

Jack Teagarden

ONE OF THE BEST LOVED & MOST ADMIRED MUSICIANS IN **JAZZ** HISTORY.

Avenger Field

NEAR **SWEETWATER** WAS THE ONLY **ALL-WOMAN** TRAINING AIR BASE IN HISTORY. DURING WORLD WAR II, IN 1943-44, 2500 WOMEN APPLIED FOR TRAINING THERE, BUT ONLY 1074 PASSED ALL SCREENING TESTS THEN PAID THEIR OWN WAY TO SWEETWATER TO BECOME **WASPS**- WOMEN'S AIRFORCE SERVICE PILOTS.

COMMANDER JACQUELINE COCHRAN SAW TO IT THAT THESE TRAINEES LIVED A REGIMENTED LIFE AND LEARNED TO FLY THE "ARMY WAY." A LOT OF MALE PILOTS TRIED TO GET ON THE BASE BUT SO STRICT WERE THE RULES FOR ENTRY THAT THEY CALLED IT *COCHRAN'S CONVENT.*

DURING WORLD WAR II 1074 WOMEN WERE TRAINED TO BE

WASPS-Women's Airforce Service Pilots

AT AVENGER FIELD IN NOLAN COUNTY FROM 1943 TO 1944.

THEY FLEW MORE THAN 60 MILLION MILES IN 78 DIFFERENT TYPES OF AIRCRAFT IN EVERY KIND OF NON-COMBAT MISSION. SOME OF THESE MISSIONS WERE CONSIDERED TOO DANGEROUS BY MALE COMBAT FLIERS WHO CLAIMED THEY "ARE ALL RISK AND NO GLORY," SUCH AS TESTING NEW AIRCRAFT, FERRYING FIGHTERS ACROSS THE COUNTRY, TRAINING PILOTS, NAVIGATORS AND BOMBADIERS, OR TOWING TARGETS FOR LIVE GUNNERY PRACTICE.

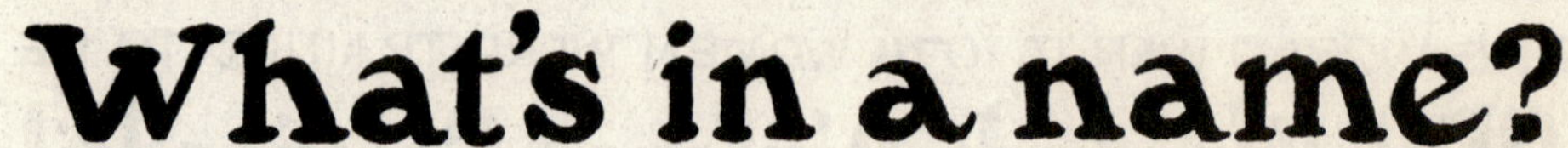

What's in a name?

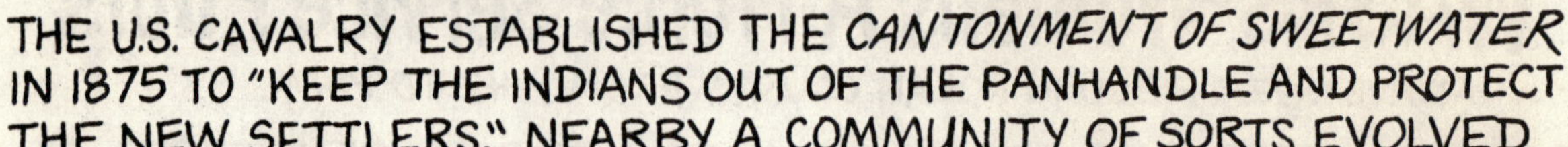

THE U.S. CAVALRY ESTABLISHED THE *CANTONMENT OF SWEETWATER* IN 1875 TO "KEEP THE INDIANS OUT OF THE PANHANDLE AND PROTECT THE NEW SETTLERS." NEARBY A COMMUNITY OF SORTS EVOLVED MADE UP OF BUFFALO HUNTERS, FREIGHTERS AND TRADERS LIVING IN TENTS. GAMBLERS, CAMP FOLLOWERS & SALOON-KEEPERS PROSPERED.

AN APPLICATION FOR A POST OFFICE WAS REJECTED IN 1879 BECAUSE THERE WAS ALREADY A *SWEETWATER* IN TEXAS.

AN INDIAN TOLD THE RESIDENTS THAT **MOBEETIE** WAS A CHEYENNE WORD FOR SWEETWATER, SO THAT'S WHAT THEY CALLED THE PLACE.

THE INDIANS HAD THE LAST LAUGH. MANY CHEYENNE CLAIM THE WORD *MOBEETIE* REALLY MEANS *BUFFALO MANURE*.